UNLOCK THE MAGIC WITHIN YOU

Tap into the Real You
and Unleash Your True Self

Dominic Beirne PhD

DISCLAIMER

The information contained in this book is for educational and informational purposes only. It is not a substitute for professional advice, diagnosis, or treatment. Always seek the advice of your doctor, therapist, or a qualified mental health professional with any questions you may have regarding a medical or psychological condition. Never disregard professional medical advice or delay seeking it because of something you have read in this book.

The author and publisher of this book make no representations or warranties with respect to the accuracy, applicability, fitness, or completeness of the contents of this book. They disclaim any warranties (expressed or implied), merchantability, or fitness for any particular purpose. The author shall in no event be held liable for any loss or other damages, including but not limited to incidental, consequential, or other damages.

This book is not intended to be a substitute for medical or mental health treatment. The information provided in this book is based on the author's personal experiences and opinions, and readers are encouraged to consult with a qualified professional before making any changes to their medical or mental health treatment. The author and publisher do not endorse any specific product, service, or treatment mentioned in this book.

CONTENTS

INTRODUCTION

Welcome to the world of self-improvement and personal growth. This book is designed to help you understand the power of your mind and how you can use it to improve your life.

In this book, we will explore various techniques and strategies that can help you achieve your goals and improve your mental well-being.

Chapter 1 will dive into the inner workings of your brain and how it affects your thoughts, emotions, and behaviour. You will learn about the different parts of the brain and how they contribute to your overall functioning.

Chapter 2 will introduce you to hypnosis, a powerful tool to help you tap into your subconscious mind and make positive changes. You will learn about the history of hypnosis and how it works.

Chapter 3 will focus on the importance of de-stressing and how you can manage stress in your life. You will learn various techniques and strategies for reducing stress and improving your well-being.

Chapter 4 will explore the connection between physical and mental health. You will learn about the mind-body connection and how to manage pain and discomfort.

Chapter 5 will focus on goal setting and how to achieve your desired outcomes. You will learn about the importance of knowing what you want and how to measure your progress.

Chapter 6 will delve into behavioural change and how to make lasting changes in your habits and routines. You will learn about the power of positive reinforcement and how to create a supportive environment for change.

Chapter 7 will introduce you to the power of affirmations and how to use them to improve your self-esteem and confidence. You will learn about different types of affirmations and how to create your own.

Chapter 8 will explore the importance of gratitude and how it can improve your mental well-being. You will learn about different gratitude practices and how to cultivate a mindset of gratitude.

Chapter 9 will focus on the power of visualisation and how to use mental imagery to achieve your goals. You will learn about different visualisation techniques and how to incorporate them into your daily routine.

Chapter 10 will provide strategies for overcoming addictions using positive thinking and self-hypnosis. You will learn about the nature of addiction and how to make positive changes in your life.

Chapter 11 summarises everything you will have learned and how it will help you lead a more fulfilling, successful life.

By the end of this book, you will have a deeper understanding of your mind and how to use it to achieve your goals and improve your mental well-being.

So, let's get started on this journey of self-discovery and personal growth!

CHAPTER 1

Understanding Your Brain

Your brain can be compared to a computer with two main parts - the conscious and the unconscious. The conscious mind is responsible for processing information and performing tasks. In contrast, the unconscious mind stores memories and experiences from the past.

Like a computer's hard drive, the unconscious is the storehouse for everything that has happened to us. It would be impossible for our conscious minds to remember everything that has ever happened to us, which is why it is all sent to the unconscious mind. That's why the unconscious is important in helping us navigate our day-to-day lives.

Imagine there are two supercomputers, one owned by Sarah and the other by Tim. Each computer has its working memory, which is in operation when Sarah or Tim are making the machine do something, and a much bigger device where all the programs are stored, including the operating system. They have a keyboard, a mouse, and usually a CD or DVD drive to interact with their machines.

The working memory is much smaller than the hard drive and focuses on immediate tasks, whereas the hard drive has lots of information that may or may not be called upon at any given moment. If there is outdated data incompatible with a new program, it can cause the system to crash. Although theoretically, one can always access stored data on the hard drive; in reality, it's sometimes difficult to find. The tasks each computer engages with and the content of their hard drives would be different because Sarah and Tim have different interests and priorities.

Now, let's call these two supercomputers Sarah's brain and Tim's brain, the working memory the conscious, and the hard drive the unconscious. The conscious mind processes information and performs tasks while the unconscious mind supplies background data from its vast store of experiences and runs the program smoothly.
Sarah and Tim use their five senses (vision, hearing, taste, touch, and smell)

as input devices to gather information from the world around them. While the brain is far more than just a computer, it's not conscious of itself as a separate entity.

Sometimes, a smell or a sound can trigger a long-forgotten memory or a powerful feeling from the unconscious mind, affecting behavior or emotions. Just like a program installed in the hard drive can affect the running of a computer. The unconscious stores everything that has ever happened to us. Some of those stored events can cause us to behave in inappropriate ways, and sometimes they can be incompatible with events happening in our current lives, leading to a crash. A phobia is an example of this - it's an irrational fear that is often caused by an event in the individual's past.

MIND MAPPING

Let's return to the analogy of Sarah and Tim and their supercomputers. Just as each computer is a unique mix of data, software, and tasks, reflecting the individuals who use it and the information they input, the same is true for Sarah and Tim's brains, which are the equivalent of supercomputers. However, unlike the basic hardware of a computer, each brain, while similar in anatomy, is unique, and each brain works dynamically. Our neural circuits can change, unlike computer circuits, which are hard-wired. As we find things that interest us and focus on those interests, we strengthen some of our neural circuits and weaken others.

Unlike computers, we can adapt and use the information we take in and apply it to new situations. We are not passive in data input; we actively seek out the things that most interest us or satisfy some need.

Now let's take a closer look at how we input data through our five senses, which are the pathways by which we obtain external sensory data and use it internally to create our own individual sense of reality.

Try this brief exercise. Close your eyes and think back to a pleasant experience from the past. Maybe it was a fantastic holiday, a success you achieved in an exam or at work, or perhaps the first date you went on with your partner. Notice how that memory first presents itself to you. Do you 'see' a picture in your mind? Or do you 'hear' the music that was playing back then? Perhaps your memory is a smell, a fragrance someone was wearing. Maybe the first thing you notice is the feeling of the sun warming your skin.

Whichever sense announces the memory to you, focus on the memory and notice the other things. See how it looks. Listen to the sounds. Breathe in and smell the smells. Allow yourself to recreate the feelings from the scene around you (such as sand under your toes, a gentle breeze) and those internal feelings of love, comfort, or happiness. You created that memory in your mind, and you did so using your five senses.

All our perceptions of the world are processed through our senses. Since each of us has different experiences and our neural network has been shaped by our interests, values, beliefs, occupations, and so on, we all end up with our unique representation of reality. This is our internal map of external reality.

Just like an ordinance survey map, which represents the terrain and not the actual territory, our internal map of reality represents it and not reality itself. And people respond to their own internal map of reality, not to reality itself. Your map is determined by how you use your senses externally and internally.

Most people have a preferred sense that they use first when inputting experience. This is known as the lead sense and significantly impacts your internal map. By becoming aware of your lead sense and paying attention to your other senses, you can alter how data is inputted. In other words, by changing the way in which you use your senses internally, you change the map.

By noticing how others perceive reality, you can adjust your behaviour to align more closely with theirs. For example, if their lead sense is visual, their internal lead sense is likely visual too. If they use expressions like "I see what you mean" or "I get the picture," their lead sense is likely visual. If they are more inclined to say, "I hear what you're saying" or "We're on the same wavelength," their lead sense is auditory. Expressions such as "Hang on a moment" or "I can't seem to get to grips with this" are used by people whose lead sense is kinaesthetic, while expressions such as "I can sniff out an opportunity a mile away" or "That stinks" are more likely to be uttered by people whose lead sense is olfactory.

By paying attention to the language people use, we can better understand their preferred sense and adjust our communication accordingly. We are on their 'wave length' or 'talking their language'. This can help improve our relationships and interactions with others.

So, how can we use this knowledge to improve our thinking and communication? One method is through the use of mind maps. They are a visual tool for organising information and ideas. They are based on the idea that the brain works by association and that visual thinking is an effective way to represent and develop ideas.

HOW TO MAKE A MIND MAP

To create a mind map, start with a central idea or topic and write it down in the centre of a blank page. Then, branch out from that central idea with related subtopics or ideas, connecting each branch to the centre with a line. From there, you can continue to add more branches and subtopics, creating a web-like structure of interconnected ideas.

The beauty of mind maps is that they allow you to see the relationships between ideas and information and to organise them in a way that makes sense to you. They can help you remember information more efficiently, generate new ideas, and solve problems. And because mind maps are visual, they can communicate ideas and information to others clearly and concisely.

Our brains are like supercomputers that take in and process information through our five senses. Our experiences and interests shape our neural network and create our unique internal map of external reality. By becoming aware of our lead sense and paying attention to the other senses, we can alter how we input data and change our internal map. Mind maps are a useful tool for organising information and ideas and for communicating them to others visually and effectively. By understanding how our brains work, we can improve our thinking and communication skills and, ultimately, our lives.

THE NERVOUS SYSTEM

Our bodies are intricate electrical machines. Every message and communication in our bodies is transmitted as electrical impulses. For instance, when we move our hand, an electrical impulse travels from the brain down a nerve to the muscles in our hand and stimulates them to contract. Similarly, the electrical activity in our hearts and brains can be measured using an ECG and EEG.

Nerves are similar to electrical wires and are insulated with a fatty sheath. However, when they reach their destination, they are not connected like electrical cables with a connector or twisted together and wrapped in insulating tape. Instead, a gap exists between the end of one nerve and the beginning of the next or between the nerve and the muscle it needs to stimulate. The electrical impulse is transmitted over this gap using chemical transmitters. Think of a battery. In a battery, chemical agents hold and share the electrical charge. Certain chemicals are excellent electrical transmitters, and this transmission is called the synapse. Millions of synapses are always active, with more occurring in our brains than anywhere else.

When we want to move our hand, for instance, a message enters our brain, either from an external source through one of our senses or from a thought that arises in the brain itself, which initiates the desire to move. The brain sends an electrical signal down the appropriate muscle group, and we move. This all happens so quickly that we are not conscious of the individual steps. Sometimes moving can be even quicker, such as when we touch something hot. Our hand moves back in a reflex action, which bypasses the brain and sets up a specialised synapse in the spinal cord to save valuable time.

Now think about how we learn. Take learning to drive. When we first start, we are very conscious of the pedals, steering, and other actions involved. Maintaining that level of awareness can be exhausting. However, the more experience we get, the easier it becomes. Eventually, the movements become automatic, and we can drive without thinking about it. The synaptic connections needed to drive become automatic. We can even drive and hold a conversation or listen to the radio without any issues. These synaptic patterns are set up below the conscious level, allowing us to make progress without being overwhelmed consciously.

We have sensory nerves that enter external data into our system and motor nerves connected to our internal map.
The way people move, or the body posture they adopt, can tell us a lot about the internal processes that are taking place.

Our motor system also helps us with internal imaging and remembering. For example, if we are asked which way our front door opens from the outside, we can access that information by opening the door in our imagination, and the appropriate hand moves to help us find the answer.
However, many things our bodies do are beyond our conscious control.

CONCLUSION

The brain can be compared to a computer with two main parts - the conscious and the unconscious. The conscious mind processes information and performs tasks, while the unconscious mind stores memories and experiences from the past. Like a computer's hard drive, the unconscious mind is the storehouse for everything that has happened to us, and it helps us navigate our day-to-day lives. Our brain's neural circuits can change dynamically, unlike a computer's hard-wired circuits. We actively seek out the things that most interest us, and our internal map of external reality is determined by our unique representation of reality based on our experiences, interests, values, beliefs, and occupations. By becoming aware of our lead sense and paying attention to our other senses, we can alter how data is inputted, which can change our internal map of reality. By noticing how others perceive reality, we can adjust our behavior to align more closely with theirs.

CHAPTER 2

Understanding Hypnosis

Although not all the techniques in this book rely on a hypnotic 'trance,' getting comfortable and relaxed is a starting point for most of them. Therefore, it's appropriate to include some information on hypnosis.

So what is hypnosis, and what are some common misconceptions? Let's dispel some myths:

1. A hypnotist can hypnotise you against your will.

This is not true. A person must be willing to be hypnotised at the conscious and unconscious level to enter into a trance state. Hypnosis cannot be forced on someone who doesn't want to be hypnotised.

2. A hypnotist can make you do things you wouldn't normally do.

Also not true. Under hypnosis, no one will do anything contrary to their moral or ethical beliefs. Nor will they do anything to make themselves look foolish unless they want to. Anyone who gets up on stage at a show to be hypnotised is willing to go along with whatever the stage hypnotist asks them to do.

3. A hypnotic trance is an unnatural state of mind.

This is not true either. Contrary to popular belief, a 'trance state' is not an abnormal state of mind that certain people can induce in others. In fact, the ability to go into hypnosis naturally is part of human behaviour.

Daydreaming is a type of hypnotic trance. If you are a car driver, you may have arrived at your destination without conscious memory of the journey. We often refer to this as being 'on automatic pilot.' We have actually been in a mild trance state. We would have snapped out of it immediately had anything untoward happened. Therefore, 'trance' states are quite normal and can happen spontaneously.

4. Hypnotists are all power-crazed weirdos seeking to get you under their control.

This is a common misconception. It's simply not true. Hypnotists are just like anybody else; there are good and bad in every profession. However, none of all the hypnotists I've encountered have been power-crazed.

In conclusion, hypnosis is a natural and safe state of mind that can be used to achieve a relaxed and comfortable state. It's important to dispel the myths and misconceptions surrounding hypnosis to fully understand and benefit from its uses.

A BRIEF HISTORY OF HYPNOSIS

Any discussion about hypnosis would not be complete unless we look at where it came from and how it became the respected therapeutic tool it is today.

Hypnosis has been around for a long time, although it went by different names, as you are about to discover! Although hypnosis had moments in history when it was disregarded or treated with suspicion, the oldest written record of hypnosis shows it was regarded with the same respect it is today.

The Ebers Papyrus, an Egyptian medical document dating back to 1550 BC, told of a cure brought about by a hypnotic treatment. The treatment involved the physician claiming godlike therapeutic powers, placing his hands on the head of the patient and making weird therapeutic declarations that resulted in cures.

Historical records show many powerful men practised healing like this. King Pyrrhus of Egypt, Emperor Vespasian, Francis I of France and other French kings are all known to have used hypnotic healing techniques.

Hypnosis was so popular in Ancient Egypt that Sleep Temples were set up in which the priests practised hypnosis on their patients and effected cures through suggestion. Sleep temples became very popular in Egypt. The idea spread throughout Asia Minor and, of course, to the Greeks – who knew a good thing when they saw one!

Hippocrates, popularly thought of as 'The Father of Medicine', is known to have discussed what we would think of as the role of the unconscious in the cause and cure of physical ills. He said, "The affliction suffered by the body, the soul sees quite well with the eyes shut."

The word 'hypnosis' comes from a combination of the Greek word 'hypnos', which means sleep and the Latin and Greek word 'osis', which means condition or state. In Greek mythology, there is even a God of Sleep, Hypnos.

When someone is hypnotised, they do not sleep in the sense we mean when we slumber for seven or eight hours at night in our beds. A hypnotic 'trance' is a state of deep relaxation and focus. The Greek practice of 'trance healing' was copied by the Romans. They adopted the Greek God of Medicine, Asclepius (son of Apollo), who was thought to effect cures in the sick through dreams. It was believed he induced a 'deep sleep' in his patients and controlled their pain by stroking his hand across their skin.

With the advent of Christianity, hypnosis became a secret healing art, as the established Church regarded hypnosis and 'trance' induction as witchcraft.

However, hypnosis and healing continued to flourish within the context of other cultures and faiths. We see the modern-day equivalent with Shamans, Hindus, Fakirs, Yogis, and the various Voodo cults.

Indeed there has been a tremendous increase in interest in the Eastern Philosophies within the Western world over the past 60 years, focusing on those who practise meditation of one form or another. There is very little difference, if any, between a self-induced hypnotic 'trance' and a self-induced meditative state. Despite the repression of the Church, there are references through the ages to the interplay of the mind and the body and the significance of that interplay in the disease process. For example, Avicenna, a famous Persian physician and philosopher in the 10th century, stated, "The imagination can fascinate and modify man's body, either making him ill or restoring him to health."

Oddly enough, the modern history of hypnosis doesn't begin with a physician but a clergyman (even odder given the Church's attitude towards 'trance healing')! Father Gassner was a Catholic priest living in the mid-1700s who believed (like most people in those days) that ill people (particularly those with psychological problems) were possessed by devils. He thought the devils needed to be cast out for the patient to improve. Somehow, Father Gassner convinced the Church that God was working through him and obtained its approval to 'cast out devils'. He was open

about his methods and frequently demonstrated them to physicians. These demonstrations took place in a theatrical environment. The observers would be seated around a stage. The patient waited on the stage for Father Gassner to appear.

With perfect timing, the priest would stride onto the stage wearing a long black flowing cape and brandishing a gold Crucifix high above his head.

The patient had been told beforehand that when Father Gassner touched him with the Crucifix, he would fall to the floor and remain prostrate. The priest would then instruct the patient to 'die'. During this period of 'death', Father Gassner could cast out the devils causing the illness. Once Father Gassner judged the devils gone, he would restore the patient back to 'life'.

So a hypnotic suggestion had already been introduced to the patient before the demonstration began.

Members of the audience were invited on stage after the patient had collapsed to the floor so they could examine him or her. After no pulse had been felt or heartbeat heard, they would pronounce the patient dead. Gassner would then order the demons to depart and restore the patient to 'life' - cured. Wow! Very cool.

One audience member who attended several such demonstrations was so impressed that he set out to reproduce the results and became responsible for introducing the techniques to the wider medical profession. His name was Franz Anton Mesmer. You may have heard of him.

Mesmer, also known as 'The Father of Hypnosis', gained significant recognition for his work in the field of hypnotism. So famous was Mesmer that hypnotism became known as 'Mesmerism'. Unlike his predecessor, Gassner, who attributed his patients' illnesses to demonic possession, Mesmer believed in something he called 'animal magnetism'. He proposed that there was a magnetic fluid in the air that our nervous system could absorb. According to him, blockages in the circulation of this fluid could cause illnesses. Those blockages needed to be corrected for patients to be cured.

Mesmer's techniques involved placing his patients in a tub full of water and

iron filings. Large iron rods protruded from the mixture. He also carried a magnetic rod, which he used to magnetise the patients, inducing a "crisis"

15

that usually took the form of a seizure. In his flowing robes and wielding his magnetic rod, it's no wonder that Mesmer's patients were so compliant.

Despite Mesmer's success, he was investigated by the French government in 1784 and declared a fraud. The lack of evidence presented before the Commission justified their verdict. Mesmer tried to convince the Commission that he had a secret worth knowing. He refused to reveal what the secret was. Instead, he hid its simplicity under a cloak of complicated play-acting and stage props.

Despite the government's verdict, the Marquis de Puysegur, a nobleman, was impressed with Mesmer and developed the practice of hypnotism to its more recognisable form today. Puysegur introduced 'artificial somnambulism', a trance state where the patients were quiet and relaxed, unlike Mesmer's 'crisis'.

Puysegur described three fundamental features of Mesmerism, focusing the patient's senses on the operator, accepting suggestions without question, and amnesia for events in a trance. These principles are recognised today by hypnotists.

In 1814, a charismatic Luso-Goan Catholic priest, Abbé Faria, realised that Mesmerism was not due to animal magnetism but to the power of suggestion. He renamed it 'somnambulism' or 'lucid sleep'.

Despite some showy demonstrations of his work in Paris, the Catholic Church was unimpressed and even accused him of dabbling in witchcraft. He was discredited but not defeated. Before he died, he published 'De la Cause du Sommeil Lucide, ou Etude de la Nature de l'homme' ('On the Cause of Lucid Sleep in the Study of the Nature of Man'), which, although derided in the 19th century as the work of a charlatan has since been recognised as a valuable resource in the hypnotic field.

James Braid, a surgeon from Manchester, England, was introduced to Mesmerism in 1841 renamed it "Hypnotism" a year later, and attempted to change it again to "Monoideism" later in life. However, the terms 'hypnotism' and 'hypnosis' had become too well known. They remain in use to this day.

Braid made several noteworthy observations about hypnosis but believed its use should be restricted to medical and dental professionals. Today, most hypnotists recognise hypnotism as a powerful tool that can be used in various contexts.

John Elliotson, a renowned physician and surgeon in England, was one of the earliest adopters of hypnotism. In 1846, he published the first journal devoted to the principles and practice of hypnotism, called Zoist. The journal featured articles from the leading physicians and surgeons of the day, including James Esdaile, who became famous for performing surgical procedures using only hypnosis for anaesthesia.

For 13 years, the journal showcased the excellent results of hypnotic treatment in various conditions, including insanity, headaches, asthma, and much more. With Elliotson's pedigree as a Professor of Medicine at London University, President of the Royal Medical and Surgical Society, and one of the founders of the University College Hospital in London, Zoist's contributions were highly regarded.

Throughout Europe and America, hypnosis as a medical therapy gained popularity, effectiveness, and a reputation of standing. However, Sigmund Freud's contributions to understanding the human mind and mental disorders caused hypnosis to fall out of favour. Freud was initially attracted to the work of a highly regarded physician and skilled hypnotist, Josef Breuer, who used hypnosis to uncover and release repressed emotions caused by past experiences. Together, they wrote a book called Studien über Hysterie.

Despite Freud's use of hypnotic techniques, such as promoting the use of his patients' imaginations, encouraging relaxation, and touching their foreheads, he eventually preferred psychoanalysis and free association. His attitude toward hypnosis as a clinical tool and his denunciation of it caused people to think of hypnosis as only a therapy of 'direct suggestion'.

As a result, hypnosis and psychoanalysis were seen as being in direct conflict. Hypnosis was considered the lesser therapy because it was believed only psychoanalysis could uncover the underlying symptoms of a patient's trauma.

However, hypnotists argue that hypnosis is an excellent analytical tool which, in addition to uncovering traumas, provides patients with a means of restructuring and rebuilding themselves. Conventional psychoanalysis, a non-directive therapy, may lead to understanding the cause without showing the patient how to put themselves back together. Furthermore, psychoanalysis is slower and more cumbersome than hypnosis in uncovering the significant traumatic event, often taking years for the patient to understand fully.

Despite being abandoned by most neurologists due to Freud's influence, some far-sighted practitioners such as Moll and Bramwell of Great Britain, Pavlov in Russia, Morton Prince and McDougall of the United States, and Pierre Janet of France continued to use hypnotism. It began to emerge once again from its relative obscurity during World War I.

Today, hypnosis is a respected therapeutic tool used to treat a wide range of conditions, from anxiety and depression to chronic pain and addiction.

SOME SIMPLE SELF HYPNOSIS TECHNIQUES

When practising self-hypnosis, you must give yourself certain suggestions to ensure a safe and effective experience. Consider the following simple techniques:

1. Always remind yourself that you can return to full awareness whenever you need or want and that you will feel completely normal.

2. Ensure that you are not under hypnosis while driving or operating machinery.

3. Strive to achieve a balance between your conscious and unconscious mind so that any suggestions you make are readily accepted by your unconscious mind.

4. With regular practice, you will find it easier to enter a state of hypnosis.

5. If you use self-hypnosis before going to bed, you can suggest to yourself that you will wake up feeling refreshed, alert, and ready for the new day at a specific time.

You can read these suggestions aloud before beginning your self-hypnosis session or record them and play the recording as you enter into a hypnotic state. Either way, these simple techniques can help enhance your self-hypnosis experience.

PROGRESSIVE RELAXATION

Progressive relaxation is a simple but powerful technique that helps you achieve a state of deep relaxation by focusing on your body's sensations. By gradually tensing and releasing your muscles, you can learn to recognise the difference between tension and relaxation and allow a soothing mental relaxation to follow.

To practice progressive relaxation, find a comfortable and quiet place where you won't be disturbed. Turn off your phone and other distractions, and ensure you're seated or lying comfortably.

1. Begin by imagining a warm wave of relaxation starting at your feet and slowly moving up your body. As the wave passes over each part of your body, it brings a deep sense of relaxation and comfort.

2. Focus on your feet, and tense the muscles for a few seconds. Notice how the tension feels in your feet, and then let the muscles go limp and relaxed as you imagine the wave of relaxation washing over them.

3. Move up to your calves, and repeat the process. Tense the muscles in your calves, hold the tension for a moment, and then release and let the muscles go limp.

4. Continue moving up through your body, tensing and releasing each set of muscles in turn. Pay attention to the contrast between the tense and relaxed states, and allow yourself to sink deeper into relaxation with each passing moment.

5. Once you've reached your face and head, take a few deep breaths and focus on breathing. Breathe in gently through your nose and out

through your mouth, imagining that you're breathing in ease and relaxation and breathing out tension and stress.

6. Take a moment to scan your body from head to toe, and notice how relaxed and comfortable you feel. You can repeat this process whenever you need to release tension and find a state of deep relaxation.

With practice, progressive relaxation can become a valuable tool for reducing stress and promoting physical and mental well-being. By tuning in to your body's sensations and using the power of your mind to release tension, you can achieve a greater sense of calm and tranquillity in your daily life.

BETTY'S SELF-HYPNOSIS TECHNIQUE

This technique, credited to Elizabeth Milton (Milton Erickson's wife), can help you enter a state of self-hypnosis to access your unconscious mind and promote relaxation.

1. Find a comfortable position, sitting or lying down, where you are unlikely to be disturbed. Remember to support your neck and head.

2. Set a time limit for your self-hypnosis session and state it out loud to yourself. For example, "I am going into self-hypnosis for 15 minutes."

3. State your intention for going into self-hypnosis. Focus on the role of your unconscious mind and how it can help you achieve your goals. For example, "I am going into self-hypnosis to allow my unconscious mind to help me with [insert your goal here]."

4. Imagine how you want to feel after the self-hypnosis session. This could be alert and refreshed, calm and reflective, or relaxed and ready for sleep.

5. Take a few moments to observe your surroundings and notice three things in the room. Focus on one object at a time, such as a doorknob or a light switch. You may choose to name each object.

6. Pay attention to the sounds in the room and identify three things you can hear.

7. Notice three sensations you can feel, such as the texture of your clothing or the comfort of the chair you are sitting in.

8. Repeat step 5, noticing two things you can see and naming them.

9. Repeat step 6, noticing two sounds you can hear.

10. Repeat step 7, noticing two sensations you can feel.

11. Repeat steps 5-7 again, this time focusing on only one thing you can see, one thing you can hear, and one sensation you can feel.

12. Close your eyes and bring an image into your mind. This could be something you actively construct or something that naturally comes to mind. Name the image.

13. Imagine a sound and name it. It could be a piece of music or the sound of the sea. If you hear external sounds, incorporate them into your internal auditory state.

14. Become aware of an internal feeling and name it. For example, "I feel a gentle breeze stirring my hair" or "I feel the warmth of the sun on my face." Incorporate external sensations into your internal state.

15. Repeat steps 12 to 14 using two internal images, two sounds, and two feelings.

16. Repeat steps 12 to 14 using three internal images, three sounds, and three feelings.

COMPLETING THE PROCESS

As you complete the process, you may find that you enter a comfortable, relaxed trance state of mind. This is a perfectly normal and beneficial outcome of the technique. Some people may even feel as though they have fallen asleep, only to find themselves returning to full awareness at the specified time. This is a sign that they were not asleep but rather in a trance state where their unconscious mind was actively fulfilling the tasks they had assigned.

If you reach the end of the process before the designated wake-up time, don't worry. Simply continue with four internal images, sounds, and feelings, then progress to five and so on.

Remember that, like all self-hypnotic techniques, the more you practice Betty's Self Hypnosis Technique, the better you will become at it. This version of the technique has been adapted by the authors from www.phillips.personal.nccu.edu.tw/hypnosis and originally appeared in In Fact Magazine.

WOODLAND WALK

1. Find a comfortable and quiet place where you won't be interrupted.

2. Set a specific time frame for your self-hypnosis session and repeat it to yourself.

3. State your purpose for entering into self-hypnosis.

4. Make positive statements to yourself about being able to come back to full awareness whenever needed, especially when driving or operating machinery.

5. Visualise how you will feel when you come back to full awareness.

6. Imagine standing in front of a little white gate that leads into a beautiful meadow with a little wood on the far side.

7. If visualising the gate is difficult, focus on feeling it with your hand or hearing its hinges squeaking in the breeze.

8. Count "one" inside your head while unlatching the gate.

9. On the count of "two", push the little gate open.

10. On the count of "three", walk through the gate.

11. On the count of "four", push the gate closed behind you.

12. On the count of "five", imagine standing on the edge of the meadow on an early summer day, feeling the warmth of the sun and a gentle breeze on your skin.

13. Take in the sights, smells, and sounds of the meadow, allowing yourself to relax deeper with every breath.

14. Step out across the meadow toward the little wood, feeling delightfully surprised at how each step takes you deeper into a relaxed state of mind.

15. Notice a path leading down into the well-spaced-out wood, with sunlight

filtering through the trees and making dappled patterns on the ground.

16. As you step onto the path, each step takes you deeper and deeper into a hypnotic state of mind.

17. Follow the sound of running water until you reach the bank of a little stream, and take in the sights and sounds around you.

18. Watch as fish snatch at insects on the surface of the clear water, and notice how the ripples they leave behind deepen your sense of relaxation.

19. Walk along the stream, admiring the butterflies and dragonflies.

20. Rest in a clearing with soft, springy grass and enjoy this calm, safe place while in a pleasant hypnotic state.

21. Take three deep breaths, each one slower than the last, and choose a word that represents this place of calm and peace.

22. Touch your wrist and repeat the chosen word to yourself, saying, "Whenever I want this calm, relaxed state of mind, I return to this place by taking three deep breaths, mentally repeating (word), and touching my wrist, and I immediately become calm, relaxed, and full of a sense of well-being."

23. Enjoy this hypnotic state of mind until the time you set for yourself to come back to full awareness.

Remember, the more you practice this self-hypnosis technique, the easier and more effective it will become.

CONCLUSION

Hypnosis is a safe and natural state of mind that can be used to achieve relaxation and comfort. Many misconceptions exist about hypnosis, such as the belief that a hypnotist can force someone to do things against their will or that being in a hypnotic trance is an unnatural state of mind. However, hypnosis has a long history and has been used as a healing tool for thousands of years. Although hypnosis faced repression from the church, it continued to thrive in other cultures and faiths. Today, hypnosis is widely used in therapy and can help people overcome a variety of issues. By understanding and dispelling the myths and misconceptions surrounding hypnosis, people can fully benefit from its uses.

CHAPTER 3

De-stressing

Stress has been labelled the modern scourge due to its association with various conditions. It is impossible to completely rid ourselves of stress, and it would not be beneficial. The physiological changes in our bodies in response to external stimuli are part of our normal defence mechanisms. They play a significant role in learning about and adapting to the environment. Our immune system and stress response system are also integrally connected. A little bit of stress keeps us alert and on our toes in certain situations, while too much stress can lead to paralysis by fear.

The body's initial response to stress is to activate the adrenal glands. They are small and triangular glands situated on top of the kidneys that manufacture and excrete three hormones - adrenaline and noradrenaline from the medulla and cortisol from the cortex. These hormones act as neurotransmitters for the sympathetic nervous system.

Adrenaline is the neurotransmitter concerned mostly with harmful stress, while noradrenaline is associated with pleasant stress. Large amounts of noradrenaline are released during exercise, leading to the release of endorphins in the brain that create a high feeling and deaden the body's response to pain. Cortisol is also released during exercise and is the body's natural anti-inflammatory. However, overtraining or constant stress can negatively impact the overall immune system, reducing the number of white blood cells.

Adrenaline is the "fear, flight, or fight" hormone. A sudden release of adrenaline readies the body for action, dilating the pupils, and increasing heart rate, blood pressure, and breathing rate. The body diverts blood from the skin to the muscles, causing a pale, cold appearance. In extreme situations, the gut may rid itself of its contents, and the bladder and rectum may let go. The body releases sugars and fats from its stores, providing nutrients to the muscles for energy production.

In conclusion, it is impossible to avoid stress altogether, and some stress is beneficial. However, it is crucial to recognise and manage stress to maintain overall health and well-being.

SAFE PLACE STRESS MANAGEMENT

1. Begin by relaxing using your favourite technique from Chapter Two.

2. Take a deep breath in, and as you exhale, say the following three words aloud: "CALM, TRANQUIL, QUIET." Repeat these words slowly and evenly, noticing how calming and comforting they feel. Imagine stretching them out like a piece of velvet. Now, release all the air from your body with a sigh and continue with deep, slow, even breaths.

3. Imagine a 'safe place', whether real or imaginary, that brings feelings of safety and calmness. Enjoy being in this place, using your senses to see it, hear it, and feel it. Allow yourself to relax even more in this space.

4. Pay attention to where you feel the pleasant emotions the safe place gives you in your body. Focus on those good feelings and intensify them.

5. Think of a word that represents your safe place and those good feelings.

6. Clear your mind for a moment, and then imagine your safe place together with your keyword. Notice how those good feelings flood your mind and body again.

7. Think of a minor annoyance that irritates you.

8. Think of your safe place once again, together with your keyword, and be delighted with how easily you can dispel those irritated feelings.

9. Repeat step 8, thinking of another minor annoyance, and notice how quickly you can transform those uncomfortable feelings into a calm state of relaxation.
Remember that this exercise is designed to help you replace stressful feelings with a calm and ordered state of mind. With practice, you can use your safe place and keyword in any stressful situation to regain a sense of peace and calm.

CONCLUSION

In summary, stress is an inevitable part of life, and our bodies are equipped with defence mechanisms to handle it. However, too much stress can have negative impacts on our immune system and overall health. The adrenal glands play a significant role in the body's response to stress, manufacturing and excreting hormones such as adrenaline, noradrenaline, and cortisol. These hormones prepare the body for action, but excessive amounts can cause harm. It is important to recognise the signs of stress and manage it effectively to maintain overall well-being. By doing so, we can ensure that stress does not become a modern scourge and instead remains a manageable part of life.

CHAPTER 4

And It Hurts Here, Doctor…

UNDERSTANDING PAIN

The first thing to know about pain is that it is there for a purpose. It's a system warning. And it's a good idea to take notice if you don't want to have a system crash! That applies to all pain, whether it be specifically from a physical source or pain that is really coming from the unconscious mind.

So Golden Rule Number One: If you develop pain of an unusually intense nature or if you experience pain that goes on for more than a day or two - always seek medical advice.

Let's say you've seen the doctor who says you've got arthritis. Or you're experiencing a migraine, or you've got an ulcer, a slipped disc, or tension headaches.

Time for Golden Rule Number Two: Follow your doctor's advice. If your doctor suggests rest, rest. If your doctor suggests medication – take it. If he wants you to go for investigations - go. Now you might think that's strange advice from a book about helping yourself. But you must deal with whatever is causing the pain immediately.

But what if your doctor tells you he can't find a physical cause for your pain? You come away feeling all dissatisfied, don't you? You tell yourself that the doctor thinks you're a hypochondriac - or worse, you're swinging the lead! Or maybe you don't believe him and embark on a round of seeking other opinions. Because there must be a cause. The pain is real. You can feel it. Yes, the pain is real, and you feel it. But this pain is coming from your unconscious. It is what doctors call psychosomatic pain. It's your unconscious mind saying: "Hey, listen to me. I need some help here." That's what psychosomatic means - the mind - psycho - affecting the body - soma! You can't divide the mind and the body.

Most people think they live in their heads. But their head and brain are as much a part of the body as anything else. The whole system interacts all the time. What goes on in the body in terms of hormones and chemicals affects the entire body - including the brain. And what goes on in the brain affects the whole body. The unconscious is a function of the brain. So the

unconscious will use the usual channels to get us to sit up and take notice. And one normal channel is the production of pain. So, sometimes, that's what it does. Unfortunately, the unconscious can't give the pain it produces a unique identifying factor. You don't sit bolt upright in bed and exclaim: "Goodness me, that unpleasant sensation in my left big toe has all the hallmarks of the unconscious. I'd better go see a therapist."

The unconscious is stuck with the same experience of pain as the rest of the body. The pain might manifest as backache, stomach ache, or headache. So, for simplicity, let's divide pain into two main categories. Pain with a known physical cause and pain without any demonstrable physical cause - psychosomatic pain. It is worthwhile stating here, however, that even if there is a demonstrable physical cause for the pain, the psyche always gets involved in the end.

The following section seems to be the same as the previous section....

PAIN MANAGEMENT TECHNIQUES

Recording these directions on a tape recorder can help you relax, listen, and follow the instructions without having to refer back to the book. In step 3, you may want to record your favourite relaxation method.

THE CONTROL PANEL

The Control Panel is a simple yet effective technique for reducing and managing pain.

1. Find a comfortable place where you can relax without interruptions.

2. Focus on the pain, paying attention to where you feel it, its intensity, and quality, such as sharp, dull, or throbbing.

3. Relax using your preferred relaxation technique (see Chapter 2)

4. Focus on the area where you typically experience the pain. Start counting from one to 10, and with each number, become aware of the pain intensifying.

5. When the pain reaches its peak, start counting down from 10. You will notice your own healing intelligence decreasing the pain as the numbers decrease. When you reach zero, say the words "calm and free" and notice that the pain has vanished. Congratulations, you did it!

6. Imagine a control panel in your brain. This panel has various buttons and switches that control different parts and functions of your body, such as your blood pressure, heart rate, breathing, and digestion. In the middle of the panel is a large knob or a sliding scale numbered from zero to 10. This knob or scale is what you'll use to manage your perception of pain.

7. Each number on the knob or scale represents a degree of pain, with 10 being the most severe and zero being completely calm and pain-free.

8. Take note of the current number on the knob or scale. Begin counting upward from that number, and with each count, imagine turning the knob or sliding the scale to that number. You will feel the pain increasing until it reaches its peak at 10.

9. Now count backwards, imagining yourself turning the numbers down as you do so. Notice the pain diminishing with each number. When you reach zero, say "calm and free" and enjoy the feeling of relaxation and being free from pain.

10. Repeat the exercise several times, turning the numbers up to increase the pain and then back down to make it disappear. Remember to count the numbers in your head as you do so. Practice this technique until you can do it anytime you want.

11. Congratulations, you're in control. It was easy, wasn't it? If pain strikes, picture the control panel in your mind, with the pain control knob or scale in the middle, and turn the pain down. Surprisingly easy, really.

SWITCHES AND WIRES:
A SIMPLE TECHNIQUE FOR PAIN CONTROL

This technique is simple yet effective in reducing pain perception.

1. Find a comfortable spot where you won't be disturbed.

2. Take a moment to focus on the pain. Where is it located? How intense is it? What kind of pain is it?

3. Use your preferred relaxation technique to ease into a relaxed state.

4. Imagine that you have a row of switches in your head. Can you see them? Great.

5. Picture a coloured light over each switch, with each light being a different colour.

6. Observe that each switch is connected to a wire that runs all the way to the part of your body where you feel the pain.

7. Take note of the colour of the light over the switch connected to the part of your body where you feel the pain. Remembering the colour will help you recall the exact switch. Ensure that the switch is turned on.

8. Focus on the part of the body where the pain is located. Try to intensify the pain and feel it more acutely.

9. Here's the trick: flick the switch up to turn it off. As you do so, the light over the switch will go out, and the pain will disappear too. It's a more comfortable feeling, isn't it?

10. To turn the pain back on, switch the switch back on, and observe the light coming back on and the pain returning.

11. Practice turning the switch on and off.

12. Whenever you need to control pain, picture the row of switches in your mind and locate the switch corresponding to the part of your body where you feel the pain. Flick the switch off, and enjoy the relief.

Remember, you can connect the switches to any part of your body that needs pain relief. Note which switch is connected to which part of your body by remembering the colour of the light over each switch.

VISUALISING THE PAIN

This technique involves using your imagination to picture what your pain looks like.

1. Find a comfortable, quiet place where you won't be interrupted.

2. Think about your pain - where it's located, how it feels, and how intense it is.

3. Use a relaxation technique that works for you to help you relax.

4. Visualise your pain. What colour is it? What shape and size is it? It could be a bright red ball or any other shape you choose.

5. Push the shape away from your body and into the space around you, about 10 feet away from your body.

6. Gradually make the shape larger and then smaller until it's the size of a pea. Then, allow it to grow to whatever size it wants to be.

7. Change the shape's colour to a lighter or completely different colour.

8. Finally, bring the shape back inside your body where the pain is located.

9. Notice how the pain feels now. You should feel more comfortable and relaxed.

Remember, you can use this technique anytime, anywhere, where it is safe to do so, to help alleviate your pain.

VISUALISING YOUR BODY'S HEALING POWER

This technique can help you tap into your body's own healing potential, empowering your inner army to fight against pain or illness. By visualising your white cells as a powerful force, you can mobilise them to take on any challenge.

1. Find a comfortable, quiet space where you won't be disturbed.

2. Focus on the pain or illness you're experiencing. Take note of where it is, how it feels, and how intense it is.

3. Use your preferred relaxation method to calm your mind and body.

4. Imagine your white cells as a mighty army. Picture them in whatever way feels most powerful to you. Are they knights on horseback or perhaps a swarm of piranha fish?

5. As the commanding officer, send out your army to the heart of the issue.

6. Visualise the pain or illness as a shape or colour, and direct your troops to surround it. As they do, watch as the pain begins to soften, smooth out, and change colour. Feel the area relaxing.

7. Hold onto this image as the pain diminishes and your body heals itself.

Whenever you need relief from pain or illness, picture your army of white cells and allow your body's natural healing abilities to take over.

Take a moment to congratulate yourself on your newfound power, and go on to live your life with renewed vitality.

COMMUNICATING WITH PAIN

Engaging in a mental dialogue with your pain can be like seeking guidance from your inner self. Pain has emotional components that you can explore through conversation. It's crucial to listen to what it says and take its advice, as it knows more about its purpose than you do.

1. Find a quiet and comfortable place where you won't be disturbed.

2. Think about your pain, where you feel it, its intensity, and its characteristics, such as sharpness or dullness.

3. Relax using your preferred relaxation method.

4. Visualise your pain as an object or even a person, creating a clear and vivid image in your mind.

5. Ask your pain why it's there, what message it has for you, and what purpose it's serving. Listen attentively to its responses.

6. Inquire about how you can alleviate the pain, taking note of its answers. If the pain is a serious bodily warning, reassure it that you will seek medical attention as soon as possible, but ask it to let you function normally until then.

7. Open your eyes and follow the pain's advice, noticing how the pain decreases.

Give yourself a pat on the back! By following this technique, you've reduced your pain and gained insight into your inner feelings.

Experiment with these methods and have fun! Once you've found one that works for you, practice it regularly until it becomes second nature. Soon, you'll find that the image pops up automatically in your mind, giving you control and putting you back in the driver's seat. It's a small mental exercise that pays off in the long run!

CONCLUSION

Pain is a warning system that should not be ignored. Seeking medical advice is essential if the pain is unusually intense or lasts for more than a day or two. Following the doctor's advice, whether it involves rest, medication, or investigations, is crucial to addressing the underlying cause of the pain. Psychosomatic pain, which comes from the unconscious mind, can manifest as physical pain without a demonstrable physical cause. Pain management techniques such as the Control Panel can be helpful in reducing and managing pain by using the mind's healing intelligence. Practice and persistence can lead to better pain control, and by following the Golden Rules, anyone can take steps towards a healthier and pain-free life.

CHAPTER 5

What Do You Want? And How Do You Know When You've Got It?

Sometimes, we may feel something is wrong or missing in our lives. We may believe we know what we want and set out to obtain it, only to find disappointment or frustration once we reach our destination. This can lead to the 'out of the fire into the frying pan' syndrome.

So, where did we go wrong? The answer lies in not working out what we truly want. Perhaps we didn't ask ourselves the right questions or ask them correctly.

Many people begin by telling themselves things like, "I have a problem", "I don't like my current situation", "My life is all wrong", or "What is my problem?" Starting with negative statements or questions leads to asking why you have the problem and who is to blame for it. You might find yourself blaming others in your life or beating yourself up. However, none of this helps bring about change or move forward.

So the first question to ask yourself is: What do I really want? Is this goal something you want, or is it something you need? Is it something you wish to possess, or is it a change in your relationships or perhaps a change of career? Do you maybe want to work differently, or is this goal more internal, involving a change in how you feel, think, or behave? When you have found the goal (or desired state) you are aiming for, it is time to ask yourself specific questions about it. As you work through these questions, you are formulating a plan – you are being creative in achieving a result, and the goal ceases to be a goal and becomes an OUTCOME – the result of a positive process for change.

Firstly always express what you want in the positive. Rather than say, "I want to give up smoking", say, "I want to become free from tobacco." Make a list of the positive things achieving your goal will do for you – in this instance, being healthier, having more money, etc. Be precise about the goal. Go over the fine details in your mind. Are there smaller goals that you need to achieve along the way? Set a time limit – and if this goal is to be achieved in stages, set the interim time limits. Is this goal appropriate in all situations and with everyone in your life, or does it only apply in certain situations or with certain people?

The more you know about your goal, the more you become aware of resources and opportunities to move you towards it. Ask yourself what you must do to achieve your goal - plan the steps. Also, ask yourself if achieving what you want also requires some action from other people and who those people are.

If it does require the help of others, how will you get them to want to help you? You are more likely to succeed if they get something positive from their actions too. If you achieve what you want, how will this benefit them?

Consider the resources you already have that can aid you in achieving your goal. People, money, training, and skills are all valuable resources to draw upon. Observe those who have already accomplished what you desire and learn from their strategies. Determine if there are any skills or training that you need and make a plan to acquire them. Also, recognise your inner qualities and how they can support you in reaching your goal. Take stock of the positive aspects of your current situation and consider how you can leverage them to help your progress towards your desired state while preserving them for the future.

Reflect on the potential outcomes of achieving your goal for yourself and others. Will sacrifices be required, such as relocating your family to a new place? Consider how these changes may impact your loved ones, friendships, and work relationships. Ensure you're prepared for any adjustments that may need to be made and that those around you are on board with your plans.

Assess how this goal aligns with your other life goals, values, and beliefs. The more interconnected your goals are, the more motivated you will be to achieve them.

How will you know when you have achieved your desired outcome? Without a clear understanding of what success looks like, it can be difficult to know when to stop striving. Feedback is crucial in providing insight into your progress.

As discussed in Chapter One, we gather information through our senses and use it to build our internal map of the world. Imagine yourself in possession of what you want. What do you see, hear, and feel? What external evidence indicates that you have achieved your goal? For example, if your objective was to manage your weight, perhaps people will notice that you look healthier. If it was to get a promotion, your new job title might appear on a plaque outside your office.

Are there interim feedback points that signify you're on the right track? Consider role-playing your desired outcome to precisely understand what it entails. As you do so, assess whether it aligns with your sense of identity. If it fits comfortably, you have identified your outcome and can begin to formulate an action plan to achieve it. Determine your first step and take it. You are now on your way to achieving your goal.

TO SUMMARISE THE STEPS

1. Identify what you truly desire.

2. Frame your desire in positive language.

3. Be specific and detailed about what you want.

4. Determine the necessary actions you need to take.

5. Identify the resources you need to achieve your goal.

6. Consider the potential consequences of achieving your goal.

7. Ensure that your goal aligns with your overall life plan and values.

8. Establish how you will recognise when you have reached your goal.

9. Confirm that your goal is in line with your personal identity.

10. Take action and get started on your journey towards your desired outcome.

CONCLUSION

The key to achieving our goals is to first work out what we truly want. This involves asking ourselves the right questions, expressing our goals in a positive manner, and being precise about what we want to achieve. It is also important to consider the resources we already have at our disposal, as well as those we may need to acquire. Additionally, we must reflect on the potential outcomes of achieving our goal and how it aligns with our other life goals, values, and beliefs. Finally, having a clear understanding of what success looks like and gathering feedback along the way is crucial in achieving our desired outcome. By following these steps and formulating a plan, we can turn our goals into outcomes and successfully achieve positive change in our lives.

CHAPTER 6

Having The Behaviour You Want

Of all the things that we can achieve in life, improving our behaviour is perhaps one of the most challenging. It requires a willingness to change and a commitment to personal growth. It often involves confronting aspects of ourselves that we may not be comfortable with. The benefits of improving our behaviour can be immense, including better relationships, greater self-esteem, and increased success in our personal and professional lives.

Fortunately, with the help of what is known as Neuro-Linguistic Programming (NLP), it is possible to develop or improve new behaviours. The New Behaviour Generator (NBG) is a powerful NLP technique that enables individuals to create and embed new behaviours within themselves.

NBG is a technique developed within Neuro-Linguistic Programming (NLP) by Richard Bandler and John Grinder.

These two men were the co-founders of NLP, which emerged in the 1970s as a method for studying and modelling human behaviour and communication. Their work in NLP has influenced psychotherapy, education, business, and personal development.

Bandler and Grinder's book Frogs into Princes is a classic NLP text and provides an overview of many NLP techniques, including the NBG. The book outlines how the NBG can create new, more beneficial, effective behaviours and habits.

Since the publication of Frogs into Princes, the NBG has been widely used by NLP practitioners and individuals interested in personal development. The technique has proven effective in helping individuals develop new skills and overcome limiting beliefs and behaviours.

There are many other books and resources available on NLP and the NBG. These resources can provide valuable insights into the theory and application of the technique and practical guidance on using the NBG to achieve specific goals and outcomes.

T|G is rooted in the idea that our behaviour is primarily a product of our beliefs and perceptions. We can change our behaviour by changing how we think about ourselves and the world around us. This is accomplished through a series of steps involving visualising the desired behaviour, modelling it after a role model, and embedding the behaviour within oneself.

The first step in the NBG process is to identify the behaviour that you would like to improve. It could be something as simple as being more patient or as complex as improving your leadership skills.

Once you have identified the behaviour, it is important to define it clearly and precisely. This means breaking down the behaviour into smaller, more manageable parts and thinking about what it looks like in action.

The second step is to find a role model who exhibits the desired behaviour. This could be someone you know personally, or it could be a public figure or celebrity. The key is to find someone who embodies the behaviour you are striving for and can serve as a source of inspiration and guidance.

The third step is to model the behaviour after your role model. This involves studying their behaviour, thinking about what they do differently than you, and identifying the beliefs and values that underpin their behaviour. By emulating your role model, you can adopt their behaviour as your own.

The fourth and final step is to embed the behaviour within yourself. This involves visualisation techniques to imagine yourself exhibiting and practising the desired behaviour in real-life situations. The goal is to make the behaviour a habit so that it becomes second nature.

By following these steps, the New Behaviour Generator can help individuals create or improve new behaviours. It is a powerful tool for personal growth and development. It can be applied in various contexts, from the workplace to personal relationships. With a commitment to change and a willingness to learn, anyone can use the NBG to achieve their goals and become the person they want to be.

USE THE NBG

Let's take a closer look at the process and how it works.

1. Identify the behaviour you want to adopt: Let's say you want to be more assertive in your workplace. Think about a role model who embodies

the assertiveness you wish to possess. This could be someone you know personally, a public figure, or a fictional character.

2. Identify the specifics of the behaviour: Observe your role model and note their specific behaviours, such as their body language, tone of voice, word choice, and overall demeanour. In our example, you might notice that your assertive role model speaks up in meetings, maintains eye contact, and uses direct language.

3. Visualise yourself adopting the behaviour: Close your eyes and imagine yourself in a situation where you want to be more assertive, such as a meeting or negotiation. Visualise yourself using the same body language, tone of voice, and language as your role model. Imagine the feeling of confidence and empowerment that comes with being assertive.

4. Associate into the experience: Now, imagine stepping into the body of your role model and experiencing their assertiveness as if it were your own. See through their eyes, feel what they feel, and hear what they hear. This helps you associate into the experience of being assertive and embeds it in your neurology.

5. Dissociate from the experience: Step back out of your role model's body and imagine yourself performing the assertive behaviour on your own. This helps you dissociate from your role model and begin to make the behaviour your own.

6. Reframe the behaviour: Reframe the behaviour in a positive way that resonates with you. Instead of saying, "I want to be more assertive", say, "I am confident and assertive in all situations." This helps to program your subconscious mind to believe that you already possess the behaviour you desire.

7. Test the new behaviour: Take action and test your new behaviour in real-life situations. Start small and work your way up, gradually building your confidence and comfort level. As you continue to practice, the new behaviour will become more natural and automatic, leading to lasting change.

CONCLUSION

Improving our behaviour can be a challenging but rewarding journey that requires a willingness to change and a commitment to personal growth. Fortunately, with the help of Neuro-Linguistic Programming (NLP) and the New Behaviour Generator (NBG), it is possible to develop or improve new behaviours. The NBG, developed by NLP co-founders Richard Bandler and John Grinder, is a technique that allows individuals to create and embed new behaviours within themselves. By following a series of steps involving identifying the desired behaviour, finding a role model, modelling the behaviour after the role model, and embedding the behaviour within oneself, individuals can adopt new, more beneficial, effective behaviours and habits. The NBG is a powerful tool for personal growth and development that can be applied in various contexts, from the workplace to personal relationships. With a commitment to change and a willingness to learn, anyone can use the NBG to achieve their goals and become the person they want to be.

CHAPTER 7

The Power of Affirmations

Affirmations are powerful tools that can help you change your mindset and develop a more positive outlook on life. They are simple, positive statements that you repeat to yourself regularly. Affirmations can help you focus on your goals, overcome limiting beliefs, and develop a greater sense of self-worth. This chapter will explore the science behind affirmations and provide practical tips for creating and using them.

THE SCIENCE BEHIND AFFIRMATIONS

Affirmations work by rewiring your brain. When you repeat a positive statement to yourself regularly, it can change the way you think and feel. The brain has a remarkable ability to change and adapt, a concept known as neuroplasticity. It allows you to rewire your brain by changing the patterns of neural connections.

Research has shown that affirmations can increase activity in the part of the brain that processes self-referential information, which is linked to self-esteem and self-worth. By repeating positive affirmations, you can strengthen the neural connections associated with positive self-beliefs and weaken those related to negative self-beliefs.

BENEFITS OF AFFIRMATIONS

The benefits of affirmations are numerous. Here are some of the ways affirmations can help you:

• Increase self-esteem and self-worth: Affirmations can help you develop greater self-worth and confidence.

• Overcome limiting beliefs: Affirmations can help you overcome limiting beliefs that hold you back from achieving your goals.

• Reduce stress and anxiety: Affirmations can help you reduce stress and anxiety by promoting a more positive outlook on life.

• Improve relationships: Affirmations can help you develop healthier relationships by promoting positive communication and self-worth.

• Enhance performance: Affirmations can help you enhance performance by improving self-confidence and self-belief.

CREATING AFFIRMATIONS

Creating affirmations is easy. Here are some tips for creating effective affirmations:

• Keep it positive: Affirmations should be positive statements that focus on what you want to achieve rather than what you want to avoid.

• Be specific: Affirmations should be specific to your goals and desires. For example, instead of saying, "I am successful," say, "I am a successful business owner."

• Use present tense: Affirmations should be in the present tense as if they are already true. For example, instead of saying, "I will be happy", say, "I am happy."

• Make it personal: Affirmations should be personal to you and your goals. For example, instead of saying, "Everyone loves me", say, "I am loved by those around me."

USING AFFIRMATIONS

Using affirmations is easy, but it requires consistency and repetition. Here are some tips for using affirmations effectively:

• Repeat affirmations daily: Repeat your affirmations daily, ideally several times a day. You can say your affirmations aloud, write them down, or repeat them silently to yourself.

• Use visual cues: Use visual cues, such as post-it notes or phone reminders, to help you remember to repeat your affirmations throughout the day.

• Focus on one affirmation at a time: Focus on one affirmation at a time rather than trying to use multiple affirmations simultaneously.

• Believe in your affirmations: Believe in the power of your affirmations and the positive changes they can bring to your life.

EXAMPLES OF AFFIRMATIONS

Here are some examples of affirmations you can use:

I am worthy of love and respect.

I am a confident and successful business owner.

I am healthy and strong.

I am filled with hope love

USING PRESENT TENSE

The use of the present tense is also vital in affirmations. It creates the feeling that the affirmation is already true and real in your life rather than a distant possibility. For example, instead of saying, "I will be successful", say, "I am successful". This creates a more powerful and immediate effect on your subconscious mind.

REPETITION

Repetition is another crucial element of effective affirmations. Repeating affirmations consistently helps to strengthen the neural pathways associated with the affirmations. The more you repeat an affirmation, the more deeply it is embedded in your subconscious mind.

PRACTICE CONSISTENCY

Consistency is important in affirmations. It is better to use affirmations daily for a shorter time rather than using them sporadically for more extended periods. The daily repetition of affirmations helps to establish them as a part of your daily routine and makes them a habit.

BELIEVE IN THE AFFIRMATIONS

It is important to believe in the affirmations you are using. If you don't believe what you are saying, then the affirmation will not be effective. It is essential to choose affirmations that resonate with you and feel true to you.

USE POSITIVE LANGUAGE

Affirmations should always be phrased in positive language. Avoid using negative words or phrases such as "I am not a failure". Instead, use positive language such as "I am successful".

MAKE IT PERSONAL

Finally, affirmations should be personal to you. Use words and phrases that resonate with you and your unique situation. Personalising your affirmations helps to create a stronger connection between you and the affirmation, making it more effective.

CONCLUSION

Affirmations are a powerful tool for transforming your mindset and achieving your goals. By following these guidelines, you can create effective affirmations that resonate with you and help you to manifest positive changes in your life. Remember to be consistent, believe your affirmations, and use positive language to positively impact your subconscious mind. With practice, affirmations can become a natural part of your daily routine and lead to positive and lasting changes in your life.

CHAPTER 8

The Power of Gratitude for Mental Well-Being

GRATITUDE AND POSITIVE PSYCHOLOGY

Positive Psychology is a field of study that focuses on the positive aspects of human experiences, such as happiness, well-being, and personal growth. Gratitude is a key component of positive psychology. It is associated with positive emotions, improved relationships, and overall well-being.

According to positive psychology research, cultivating gratitude can help to shift our focus from negative to positive aspects of our lives. Focusing on the positive makes us more likely to experience positive emotions like joy, contentment, and satisfaction. Additionally, when we feel grateful for the good things in our lives, we are more likely to engage in behaviours that support our well-being, such as exercising, eating well, and getting enough sleep.

Furthermore, positive psychology research has shown that gratitude is linked to resilience. When we experience challenging situations, focusing on the positive aspects of our lives can help us to cope and bounce back more quickly. Gratitude can help us reframe negative experiences more positively, improving our mood and overall well-being.

THE POWER OF GRATITUDE IN RELATIONSHIPS

Relationships are a key component of our lives, and cultivating gratitude can help to improve our relationships with others. When we express gratitude to others, we acknowledge and appreciate their contributions to our lives. This can help to strengthen our relationships with family, friends, coworkers, and romantic partners.

Expressing gratitude can also help to build trust and intimacy in our relationships. When we feel appreciated and valued, we are more likely to open up and share our thoughts and feelings with others. This can lead to deeper, more meaningful connections with the people in our lives.

Additionally, cultivating gratitude can help to reduce conflict and negativity in our relationships. When we focus on the positive aspects of our relationships, we are less likely to get caught up in disagreements and misunderstandings. Expressing gratitude can also help us to forgive and let go of past hurts, which can improve the overall health of our relationships.

GRATITUDE AND MENTAL HEALTH

The connection between gratitude and mental health is well-established in the research literature. Grateful people tend to have higher levels of positive emotions, such as happiness, contentment, and optimism, and lower levels of negative emotions, such as stress, anxiety, and depression.

One study found that writing letters of gratitude for just three weeks resulted in participants reporting higher levels of happiness and fewer symptoms of depression. Another study showed that keeping a gratitude journal for two weeks made participants more optimistic about the future.

Gratitude can also help to improve our overall well-being. Gratitude has been shown to boost the immune system, lower blood pressure, and reduce inflammation.

PRACTISING GRATITUDE

There are many ways to practice gratitude. Here are some suggestions for cultivating gratitude in your daily life:

• Keep a gratitude journal. Take a few minutes each day to write down three to five things you are grateful for. These can be big or small things, such as a sunny day, a delicious meal, or a kind gesture from a friend.

• Express gratitude to others. Take time to thank the people in your life who have positively impacted you. This can include family members, friends, coworkers, mentors, and anyone else who has helped you in some way. When you express gratitude to others, it not only makes them feel good, but it also strengthens your relationships with them.
It's important to be specific about what you are grateful for and how the person's actions have impacted you. For example, instead of just saying, "Thanks for all your help", you could say, "I really appreciate how you took the time to listen to me and offer support when I was going through a tough time."

Expressing gratitude to others can also have a positive impact on your own well-being. It can help you to focus on the positive aspects of your life and strengthen your relationships with others. When you express gratitude to others, you also acknowledge the good things in your life and reinforce a positive mindset.

In addition to expressing gratitude to others, practising self-gratitude is important. This means acknowledging and appreciating the positive aspects of yourself and your life. Self-gratitude can help to improve your self-esteem and overall well-being. It can also help you to be more resilient during challenging times.

Ways to practice self-gratitude include writing down things you are proud of, acknowledging your strengths and accomplishments, and practising self-care. Taking time to care for yourself and do things that make you happy is a way of expressing gratitude for your well-being.

Cultivating gratitude can also be done through mindfulness practices. Mindfulness is being fully present and engaged in the current moment without judgment. When we practice mindfulness, we can be more aware of our thoughts and feelings and choose to focus on the positive aspects of our experiences.

Many different mindfulness practices can help us to cultivate gratitude. One simple method is to take a few minutes each day to focus on your breath and reflect on what you are grateful for. You can also practice gratitude meditation, which involves focusing on gratitude and appreciation for a particular person or experience.

Volunteering and giving back to others is another way to cultivate gratitude. When we volunteer and help others, we can see the positive impact our actions can have on the world around us. This can help us feel more grateful for the good things in our lives and motivate us to continue to help others.

Finally, spending time in nature can also be a way to cultivate gratitude. Nature can remind us of the beauty and wonder of the world around us. By appreciating the natural world, we can cultivate a sense of awe and gratitude for the beauty surrounding us.

In conclusion, cultivating gratitude is essential to our mental health and well-being. By focusing on the positive aspects of our lives and expressing appreciation for the good things we have, we can reduce stress and anxiety, build stronger relationships, and improve our overall quality of life. There are many ways to practice gratitude, and finding the techniques that work best for you is important. Whether it's keeping a gratitude journal, expressing gratitude to others, practising mindfulness, volunteering, or spending time in nature, cultivating gratitude can be a powerful tool for improving mental health and well-being.

CONCLUSION

To summarize, positive psychology emphasizes the importance of focusing on the positive aspects of human experiences, including gratitude. Gratitude is linked to positive emotions, improved relationships, and overall well-being. By cultivating gratitude, we can shift our focus from negative to positive aspects of our lives, which can lead to increased positive emotions and engagement in behaviors that support our well-being. Gratitude also helps us to reframe negative experiences more positively, improving our mood and overall well-being. Practicing gratitude can take many forms, including keeping a gratitude journal, expressing gratitude to others, practicing self-gratitude, mindfulness practices, volunteering, and spending time in nature. By incorporating gratitude into our daily lives, we can improve our mental health, build stronger relationships, and lead happier, more fulfilling lives.

CHAPTER 9

Understanding Visualisation

Visualisation, also known as mental imagery, is the process of creating a mental image or picture of a desired outcome or goal. This technique involves using your imagination to create a vivid and detailed mental representation of your goal. Visualisation has been used for centuries by athletes, performers, and successful individuals to enhance their performance, achieve their goals, and overcome obstacles.

The concept of visualisation is based on the idea that the mind and body are interconnected and that mental images can have a powerful effect on the body's physiology and behaviour. When you visualise yourself achieving a goal, your brain activates the same neural pathways it would if you were actually performing the action. This process can help you build confidence, increase motivation, and develop a clear sense of direction towards your goals.

Visualisation can be used in various contexts, including sports, business, education, and personal development. Some common uses of visualisation include:

• Preparing for a competition or performance

• Improving focus and concentration

• Increasing self-confidence and self-esteem

• Developing a positive mindset and attitude

• Overcoming fears and anxieties

• Improving communication and relationships

• Enhancing creativity and problem-solving skills

• Improving physical health and well-being

THE SCIENCE OF VISUALISATION

The use of visualisation is based on the principle of neuroplasticity, which is the brain's ability to change and adapt in response to experiences and environmental factors. Neuroplasticity has been extensively studied in recent years. Research has shown that mental imagery can significantly impact brain function and behaviour.

One study conducted by researchers at Harvard Medical School found that mental rehearsal can lead to changes in brain activity similar to those that occur during physical practice. The study involved a group of volunteers who were asked to practice playing a simple piano melody on a keyboard for five consecutive days. One group physically practised the melody, while the other group imagined playing the melody in their minds. The researchers found that both groups showed similar changes in brain activity, indicating that mental rehearsal can be just as effective as physical practice.

Other studies have found that visualisation can positively impact various cognitive and physical functions. For example, a study published in the Journal of Applied Psychology found that athletes who used visualisation techniques before a competition showed improved performance and reduced anxiety compared to those who did not use visualisation. Another study, published in the Journal of Pain, found that patients who used visualisation techniques to manage their pain reported lower pain intensity and discomfort than those who did not use visualisation.

These studies provide evidence for the effectiveness of visualisation and support the idea that mental imagery can have a powerful impact on our thoughts, emotions, and behaviours.

THE BENEFITS OF VISUALISATION

The use of visualisation has been linked to a variety of benefits, including improved performance, increased motivation, and enhanced well-being. Some of the specific benefits of visualisation include:

1. Improved Performance: Visualisation can be a powerful tool for enhancing performance in sports, business, and other areas. You can create

a clear mental picture of success by mentally rehearsing a desired outcome.

This can help you develop the skills and strategies to achieve your goals.

2. Increased Motivation: Visualisation can help you build motivation and develop a clear direction towards your goals. By imagining yourself achieving your desired outcome, you can create a sense of excitement and enthusiasm that can propel you towards success.

3. Enhanced Well-being: Visualisation can also positively impact your mental and physical health. Visualising yourself in a positive and healthy state can create a sense of well-being and reduce stress and anxiety.

4. Visualisation can boost your creativity and problem-solving skills by allowing you to imagine various scenarios and outcomes. Visualisation exercises can help you think outside the box and develop innovative ideas and strategies to tackle challenges. This can prove particularly beneficial in professional settings where creative problem-solving skills are highly valued.

VISUALISATION AND SPORTS PERFORMANCE

Visualisation is often used by athletes to enhance their performance. Many top athletes use visualisation techniques to mentally rehearse their performance before a competition. This can help them to stay focused and confident during the actual event. Visualisation can also help athletes to improve their technique and prepare for specific scenarios, such as dealing with unexpected obstacles or opponents.

Research has shown that visualisation can be an effective tool for improving sports performance. For example, a study published in the Journal of Sports Sciences found that basketball players who used mental imagery techniques during their practice sessions significantly improved their shooting accuracy compared with those who did not use visualisation.

Another study, published in the International Journal of Sport Psychology, found that gymnasts who used visualisation techniques experienced significant improvements in their performance compared with those who did not use visualisation.

VISUALISATION AND HEALTH

Visualisation techniques can also be used to improve health outcomes. For example, visualisation can be used to reduce pain and anxiety in medical settings. Patients undergoing medical procedures or treatments can use visualisation to create mental images of a peaceful and healing environment, which can help reduce their stress and discomfort.

Visualisation can also be used to support healthy behaviours. For example, individuals trying to quit smoking can use visualisation techniques to imagine themselves as nonsmokers, enjoying improved health and vitality. Similarly, individuals trying to lose weight can use visualisation to imagine themselves as fit and healthy, enjoying an active lifestyle and more self-confident.

VISUALISATION AND PERSONAL DEVELOPMENT

Visualisation techniques can also be used to support personal development goals. By creating mental images of our desired outcomes, we can cultivate a sense of clarity and focus that can help us to take action towards our goals. For example, people looking for a new job can use visualisation techniques to imagine themselves in their ideal position, feeling fulfilled and successful. This can help to build confidence and motivation to take action towards finding and securing that job.

Visualisation can also be used to improve our relationships. By visualising positive interactions and outcomes with others, we can cultivate a sense of empathy and understanding that can help to strengthen our relationships and resolve conflicts.

HOW TO PRACTICE VISUALISATION

Now that we have explored the many benefits of visualisation, let's look at some techniques for practising visualisation.

1. Find a quiet and comfortable space where you will not be interrupted. Sit or lie down in a comfortable position.

2. Close your eyes and take a few deep breaths, relaxing your body and clearing your mind.

3. Choose an image or scenario that you would like to visualise. This can be anything from a peaceful natural setting to an important event or situation.

4. Create a vivid mental image of the scene or situation using all of your senses. Imagine what you see, hear, feel, smell, and taste.

5. Engage with the image or scenario, imagining yourself as an active participant. Visualise yourself achieving your goals or experiencing positive outcomes.

6. Stay with the visualisation for as long as you like, savouring the positive feelings and sensations. When you are ready, slowly open your eyes and return to the present moment.

7. Practice visualisation regularly, ideally daily, for best results. You can focus on a different image or scenario each time or repeat the same visualisation if it is particularly effective.

CONCLUSION:

Visualisation is a powerful technique that can help us to achieve our goals, improve our performance, and enhance our overall well-being. By using mental imagery to create positive scenarios and outcomes, we can cultivate a sense of clarity, focus, and motivation that can help us to take action towards our goals

CHAPTER 10

Overcoming Addictions: Using Positive Thinking and Self-Hypnosis

Addiction is a complex issue that affects many individuals and their families. The addictive behaviour often stems from underlying psychological, emotional, or physical issues that require professional intervention. However, there are steps that individuals can take to help overcome addictions, including using positive thinking and self-hypnosis. In this chapter, we'll explore how positive thinking and self-hypnosis can be used to overcome addictions and provide some practical tips and exercises to help you get started.

UNDERSTANDING ADDICTION

Before we delve into the strategies for overcoming addiction, it's important to understand what addiction is and how it affects individuals. Addiction is a chronic disease that affects the brain's reward, motivation, and memory functions. It is characterised by a compulsive desire to use a substance or engage in a behaviour despite the negative consequences that result from that behaviour.

Addiction can take many forms, including substance abuse (alcohol, drugs), behavioural addictions (gambling, gaming, shopping), and even addiction to negative thought patterns. Addiction often starts as a coping mechanism for dealing with stress, trauma, or other emotional issues. However, the addiction can take over a person's life over time, leading to physical, emotional, and social problems.

THE ROLE OF POSITIVE THINKING IN OVERCOMING ADDICTION

Positive thinking is a mental attitude that emphasises the positive aspects of life and focuses on finding solutions to problems rather than dwelling on the negative. Positive thinking can be a powerful tool for overcoming addiction. It helps shift the focus away from addictive behaviour towards a more positive and hopeful outlook.

Research has shown that positive thinking can benefit individuals dealing with addiction. For example, a study published in the Journal of Clinical

Psychology found that individuals who received positive psychology

interventions reported reduced levels of substance abuse and improved overall well-being. Positive thinking can also help reduce stress and anxiety, common triggers for addictive behaviour.

USING SELF-HYPNOSIS TO OVERCOME ADDICTION

Self-hypnosis is a technique that involves inducing a state of deep relaxation and heightened suggestibility to promote positive changes in behaviour or thought patterns. Self-hypnosis can be a powerful tool for overcoming addiction. It helps access the subconscious mind, where many habits and behaviours are stored.

There are several ways that self-hypnosis can be used to overcome addiction. For example, individuals can use self-hypnosis to:

• Reduce cravings: By inducing a state of deep relaxation and focusing on positive suggestions, self-hypnosis can help to reduce cravings for addictive substances or behaviours.

• Change negative thought patterns: Self-hypnosis can be used to identify and change negative thought patterns contributing to addictive behaviour.

• Increase motivation: Self-hypnosis can help to increase motivation to overcome addiction by reinforcing positive affirmations and goals.

• Manage stress and anxiety: Self-hypnosis can promote relaxation and reduce stress and anxiety, common triggers for addictive behaviour.

PRACTICAL TIPS AND EXERCISES FOR USING POSITIVE THINKING AND SELF-HYPNOSIS

Now that we've explored the role of positive thinking and self-hypnosis in overcoming addiction, let's take a look at some practical tips and exercises that you can use to get started:

1. Start with small goals: Overcoming addiction can be challenging, so it's important to start with small, achievable goals. For example, instead of trying to quit cold turkey, set a goal to reduce your substance use or addictive

behaviour by a certain percentage each week. Practice positive affirmations. They are statements that reinforce positive beliefs and attitudes. Practice saying affirmations such as "I am strong and capable of overcoming my addiction", "I am in control of my thoughts and actions", and "I choose to live a healthy and fulfilling life." Repeat these affirmations regularly, either out loud or in your head, to help reprogram your subconscious mind and reinforce positive thinking.

2. Seek support: Overcoming addiction can be difficult, but it's important to know that you don't have to do it alone. Seek help from friends, family members, or a support group. Talking to someone who understands what you're going through can be incredibly helpful and provide the motivation and encouragement you need to stay on track.

3. Use visualisation techniques: Visualisation techniques can be a powerful tool in overcoming addiction. Visualise yourself living a healthy, addiction-free life. Imagine how it would feel to be free from addiction's hold on you. By visualising the positive outcomes of overcoming addiction, you can create a sense of motivation and determination to succeed.

4. Practise self-hypnosis: Self-hypnosis is a technique that involves inducing a state of deep relaxation and using positive suggestions to change your behaviour or mindset. You can reprogram your subconscious mind and reinforce positive beliefs and behaviours by practising self-hypnosis. You can find self-hypnosis scripts and recordings online or work with a professional hypnotherapist.

5. Celebrate your progress: Overcoming addiction is a long and challenging process, so it's important to celebrate your progress along the way. Take time to acknowledge and celebrate small achievements, such as reducing substance use or attending a support group meeting. Celebrating your progress can help reinforce positive behaviours and motivate you to continue your journey.

CONCLUSION

Overcoming addiction can be challenging and complex, but it is possible with the right mindset, tools, and strategies. Positive thinking and self-hypnosis can be effective techniques for managing addiction and achieving long-term recovery. Individuals can break free from negative patterns and behaviours by focusing on positive thoughts and beliefs and using self-hypnosis to reprogram the subconscious mind.

One of the key takeaways from this chapter is that addiction is often rooted in negative thought patterns and beliefs. Individuals can shift their perspectives and create a more positive mindset by identifying and challenging these negative beliefs. Positive affirmations, visualisation exercises, and other techniques can be helpful in this process.

Self-hypnosis is another powerful tool for overcoming addiction.
By accessing the subconscious mind, individuals can uncover the root causes of their addiction and reprogram their thoughts and behaviours. With the guidance of a qualified hypnotherapist or through self-hypnosis techniques, individuals can create new, positive habits and beliefs that support their recovery.

It's important to note that overcoming addiction is not a one-time event but a process that requires ongoing effort and commitment. It's essential to seek support from friends, family, and professionals and stay committed to the recovery journey. Starting with small goals and celebrating progress along the way can help individuals stay motivated and focused.

CHAPTER 11

The Path to Mental Wellness: Putting it All Together

As we conclude this book, it is important to note that our mental well-being is a critical aspect of our lives. Our thoughts, emotions, and behaviours impact our physical and emotional health and overall quality of life. Through the chapters in this book, we have explored various techniques and strategies to improve our mental well-being and overcome common challenges such as stress, pain, and addiction.

We began by delving into the workings of our brains and understanding the power of our thoughts in shaping our experiences. From there, we explored hypnosis, a technique that can help us tap into our subconscious mind to change negative thought patterns and behaviours. We also learned the importance of de-stressing and managing pain through relaxation techniques.

Next, we focused on setting goals and understanding how to achieve them. By identifying what we truly want and using positive affirmations, we can shift our mindset to abundance and success. We also learned the power of gratitude in fostering mental well-being and building stronger relationships.

In addition, we explored the power of visualisation, which can help us achieve our goals and boost our creativity. Finally, we delved into the challenges of addiction and how we can use positive thinking and self-hypnosis to overcome them.

By incorporating these techniques into our daily lives, we can take control of our mental well-being and achieve greater success, happiness, and fulfilment. I hope this book has provided you with valuable insights and tools to improve your mental well-being and lead a more fulfilling life. Remember, the power to create positive change begins with your thoughts, so choose them wisely.

Seeking the help of a professional therapist or counsellor can be incredibly beneficial for those struggling to overcome their issues alone. While the techniques and strategies outlined in this book may be helpful, they might not be enough for everyone.

A trained therapist or counsellor can provide a safe and supportive space to explore your thoughts and feelings, identify underlying issues contributing to your struggles, and provide personalised guidance and support as you work towards your goals. They can also help you develop coping strategies for dealing with stress, anxiety, and other challenges that may arise during your journey towards greater mental well-being.

It's important to remember that seeking help from a professional does not mean you are weak or incapable of handling things on your own. In fact, it takes great strength and courage to acknowledge when you need help and take steps to prioritise your mental health and well-being.

If you are struggling with addiction or other serious mental health concerns, seeking the help of a professional is particularly important. Addiction can be a complex and challenging issue to overcome. The support of a trained therapist or counsellor can be invaluable in helping you navigate the road to recovery.

Remember, you don't have to face your struggles alone. Whether you choose to use the techniques outlined in this book or seek the guidance of a professional therapist, taking steps towards greater mental well-being is a brave and vital decision. With dedication, perseverance, and support, you can overcome even the toughest challenges and live a happy, fulfilling life.

ABOUT THE AUTHOR

Dominic Beirne is a highly qualified therapist and trainer with over 30 years of private practice experience. He has dedicated his life to helping individuals overcome their challenges and lead happier, more fulfilling lives. Throughout his career, he has developed a deep understanding of the power of the mind and its ability to heal and transform.

In addition to his extensive experience as a therapist, Dominic is also a skilled trainer with over 25 years of experience running his own training school. He is passionate about sharing his knowledge and expertise with others and has trained countless individuals to become successful therapists in their own right.

Through his work, Dominic has helped countless individuals overcome a wide range of challenges, from addiction and anxiety to stress and relationship issues. He is committed to helping people live their best lives and achieve their full potential and believes that everyone has the power to heal and transform themselves with the right tools and support.

Dominic is widely respected in his field for his work as both a therapist and a trainer. He continues to be an active member of the therapeutic community and regularly attends conferences and workshops to stay up-to-date with the latest research and techniques.

Dominic brings a wealth of knowledge, experience, and passion to this book and is committed to helping readers achieve their goals and overcome their challenges through the power of positive thinking, self-hypnosis, and other proven techniques.

HOW DOMINIC CAN HELP YOU?

GET A SPECIAL READER OFFER

As a token of appreciation for reading my book, I'm extending a special offer to you. You can now enjoy your first online therapy session at half the price! To avail this limited-time offer, simply email me at dbeirne@hypnosis-nlp.co.uk and include "Unlock the Magic Within Me" in the subject line. Don't forget to leave your name and contact number so we can schedule your session.

Printed in Great Britain
by Amazon

43760827R00036